PEARSON English Learning System

Workbook

Anna Uhl Chamot

Jim Cummins

Sharroky Hollie

PEARSON

Upper Saddle River, New Jersey • Boston, Massachusetts • Chandler, Arizona • Glenview, Illinois

Pearson Longman Cornerstone 2
Workbook

PEARSON **English Learning System**

Staff credits: The people who made up the Cornerstone team, representing editorial, production, design, manufacturing, and marketing, are John Ade, Rhea Banker, Daniel Comstock, David Dickey, Gina DiLillo, Johnnie Farmer, Nancy Flaggman, Charles Green, Karen Kawaguchi, Ed Lamprich, Niki Lee, Jaime Leiber, Chris Leonowicz, Tara Maceyak, Linda Moser, Laurie Neaman, Leslie Patterson, Sherri Pemberton, Diane Pinkley, Liza Pleva, Susan Saslow, Chris Siley, Loretta Steeves, Kim Steiner, and Lauren Weidenman.

Text composition: The Quarasan Group, Inc.

Illustrations: **N. Jo Tufts** 4-6; **Elliot Kreloff** 16-17; **Elizabeth Allen** 23, 30-32; **Diana Kizlauskas** 36; **Helen Cann** 36; **Christine Schneider** 63; **Stephen Snider** 89; **Kevin Rechin** 115-116

Photos: Unit 1: 10, Buccina Studios/Getty Images; 11, Ken Huang/Getty Images; 12 top, Royalty-Free/Corbis; 12 middle bottom, Ken Huang/Getty Images; 12 bottom, Marcin Sadlowski/Fotolia Unit 3: 57, Macduff Everton/Getty Images Unit 4: 83, Time Life Pictures/Getty Images; 84, Retrofile/Getty Images; 88, Z. Legacy Corporate Digital Archives Unit 5: 109, Howard Rice/DK Images Unit 6: 135, Darryl Balfour/Getty Images; 141, Getty Images

ISBN-13: 978-1-4284-3485-1
ISBN-10: 1-4284-3485-2

Printed in the United States of America
14 17

Contents

Unit 1

Reading 1
Vocabulary......3
Phonics.........4
Think It Over..........5
Grammar.......7
Writing.........8

Reading 2
Vocabulary......9
Phonics....... 10
Think It Over........ 11
Grammar..... 13
Writing....... 14

Reading 3
Vocabulary.... 15
Phonics....... 16
Think It Over........ 17
Grammar..... 19
Writing....... 20

Unit 1 Review
Review....... 21
Writing Workshop... 23
Fluency...... 25
Learning Checklist.... 27

Unit 2

Reading 1
Vocabulary.... 29
Phonics....... 30
Think It Over........ 31
Grammar..... 33
Writing....... 34

Reading 2
Vocabulary.... 35
Phonics....... 36
Think It Over........ 37
Grammar..... 39
Writing....... 40

Reading 3
Vocabulary.... 41
Phonics....... 42
Think It Over........ 43
Grammar..... 45
Writing....... 46

Unit 2 Review
Review....... 47
Writing Workshop... 49
Fluency...... 51
Learning Checklist.... 53

Unit 3

Reading 1
Vocabulary.... 55
Phonics....... 56
Think It Over........ 57
Grammar..... 59
Writing....... 60

Reading 2
Vocabulary.... 61
Phonics....... 62
Think It Over........ 63
Grammar..... 65
Writing....... 66

Reading 3
Vocabulary.... 67
Phonics....... 68
Think It Over........ 69
Grammar..... 71
Writing....... 72

Unit 3 Review
Review....... 73
Writing Workshop... 75
Fluency...... 77
Learning Checklist.... 79

Contents

Unit 4

Reading 1
Vocabulary.... **81**
Phonics....... **82**
Think It Over **83**
Grammar **85**
Writing....... **86**

Reading 2
Vocabulary.... **87**
Phonics....... **88**
Think It Over **89**
Grammar **91**
Writing....... **92**

Reading 3
Vocabulary.... **93**
Phonics....... **94**
Think It Over **95**
Grammar **97**
Writing....... **98**

Unit 4 Review
Review **99**
Writing Workshop.. **101**
Fluency..... **103**
Learning Checklist... **105**

Unit 5

Reading 1
Vocabulary... **107**
Phonics...... **108**
Think It Over **109**
Grammar **111**
Writing...... **112**

Reading 2
Vocabulary... **113**
Phonics...... **114**
Think It Over **115**
Grammar **117**
Writing...... **118**

Reading 3
Vocabulary... **119**
Phonics...... **120**
Think It Over **121**
Grammar **123**
Writing...... **124**

Unit 5 Review
Review **125**
Writing Workshop.. **127**
Fluency..... **129**
Learning Checklist... **131**

Unit 6

Reading 1
Vocabulary... **133**
Phonics...... **134**
Think It Over **135**
Grammar **137**
Writing...... **138**

Reading 2
Vocabulary... **139**
Phonics...... **140**
Think It Over **141**
Grammar **143**
Writing...... **144**

Reading 3
Vocabulary... **145**
Phonics...... **146**
Think It Over **147**
Grammar **149**
Writing...... **150**

Unit 6 Review
Review **151**
Writing Workshop.. **153**
Fluency..... **155**
Learning Checklist... **157**

Name ____________________ Date ____________

Vocabulary

A. Write the word that completes each sentence.

Sight Words
sing
are
buy
eat

1. They like to ________________ and clap in music class.

2. The cat and the man ________________ playing.

3. I cut the grass. It is my ________________.

4. I ________________ my face in the morning.

5. I ________________ up my messy bedroom.

B. Circle four vocabulary words in the Word Search.

A	B	U	Y	W	A	S
S	I	N	G	E	A	T
P	X	A	R	E	M	C

Unit 1

Phonics

A. Write the letters in the correct order to make a word.

1.  n h d a nan

2.  m a l p lap

3.  a c t cat

4.  t h a hat

B. Write *a, b, f,* or *s* to complete each word.

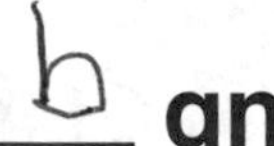

5. b an
6. f nt
7. S at
8. S ad
9. b ag
10. g ct

Name ______________________ Date __________

Think It Over

Reread to tell about the story.

Gramps has a bag of soap.

Dan can wash a sock. Dan and

Gramps can wash and clean.

A. Circle the letter of the correct answer. Then write the word.

1. Dan washes a ______________.

   a. car c. sack
   b. sock d. clean

2. Dan and Gramps wash and ______________.

   a. clean c. read
   b. dance d. buy

3. Gramps has a bag of ______________.

   a. balls c. soap
   b. books d. cans

B. Read the sentences. Think of what comes first, next, and last. Write the sentences in the correct order.

Dan and Gramps have a chore.
Dan's bag is full.
Gramps can buy a ham.

1. 

2. gra mpscan buyaham

3. 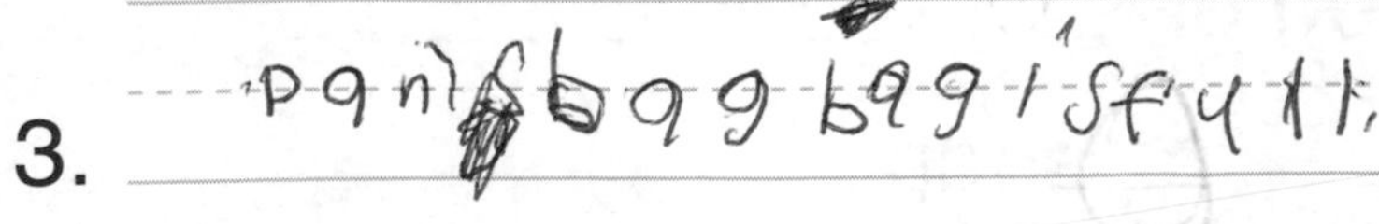

Name ______________________ Date __________

Grammar: *Can* + Verb

Use ***can*** **+ verb** to talk about things someone is able to do.

Use ***cannot*** or ***can't*** **+ verb** for things someone is not able to do.

Write *can* or *can't* to complete each sentence.

Example: Can your sister swim? No, she can't.

1. ______________ the baby play basketball?

   No, he ______________.

2. ______________ Ava ride a bike?

   Yes, she ______________.

3. ______________ tigers run?

   Yes, they ______________.

4. ______________ dogs fly?

   No, they ______________.

Writing

The paragraph below is missing four periods. Write the periods at the end of each sentence.

Anna likes to have fun. She can ride a bike
She can also swim

Anna can't play basketball very well She
cannot jump rope

Name ______________ Date ______________

Vocabulary

A. Write the word that completes each sentence.

1. My pet ______________ soft.
2. I ______________ my leg.
3. Her desk is ______________ .
4. I ______________ math in school.
5. I ______________ the pen to my dad.

Sight Words
give
big
feels
hurt

Story Words
learn
parents
children

B. Circle four vocabulary words in the Word Search.

E	N	P	A	R	E	N	T	S
C	H	I	L	D	R	E	N	P
Z	B	Q	T	L	E	A	R	N
U	D	F	E	E	L	S	Y	G

Phonics

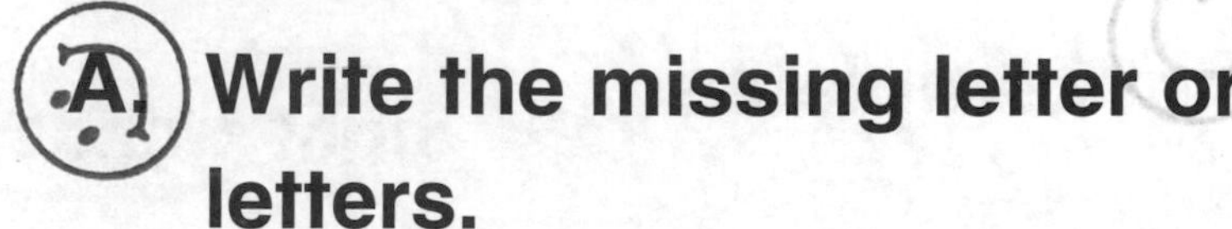

A. Write the missing letter or letters.

1. 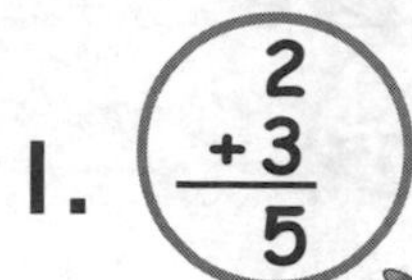

ma ____

2.  m ____ n

3. b ____ d

4.  ba ____

5.  h ____ n

B. Write *e* or *th* to complete each word.

6. w ____ b

7. ma ____

8. n ____ t

9. ____ en

10. p ____ n

Name ____________________ Date __________

Think It Over

Reread to tell about the story.

Glen is a small baby. Mom and Dad help Glen. Dad can give Glen a bottle.

Glen can be fed. Then Glen can get a nap.

A. Answer the questions.

1. Who is Glen?

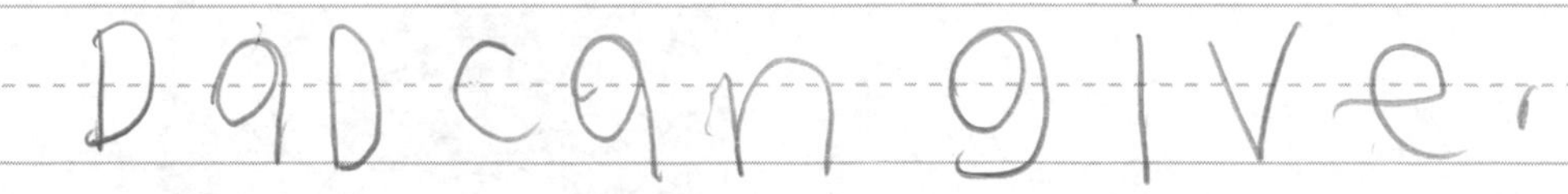

2. Who gives Glen a bottle?

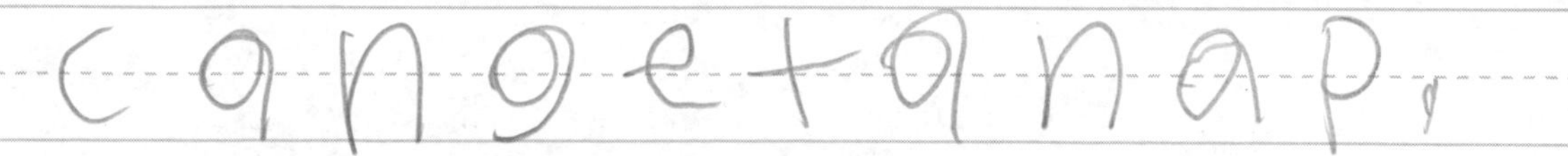

3. What can Glen do after he has his bottle?

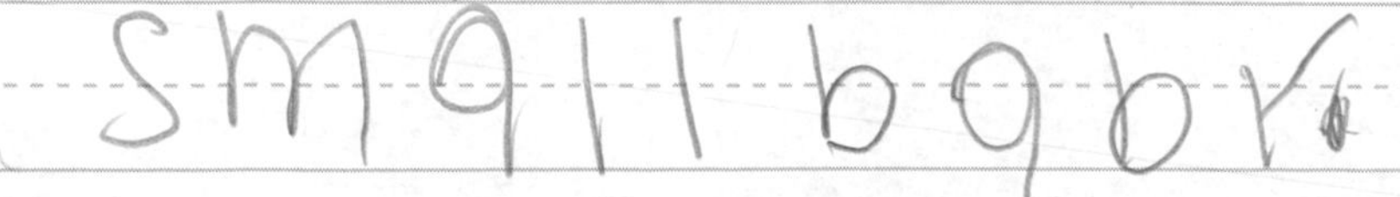

4. Why does Glen need a lot of care?

B. Match each cause with the picture that shows the effect. Write the letter of the correct answer.

1. ______ Glen can't hold his bottle.

2. ______ Bess makes a mess.

3. ______ Nell wants to eat.

4. ______ Fred has a bat.

a. 

b. 

c. 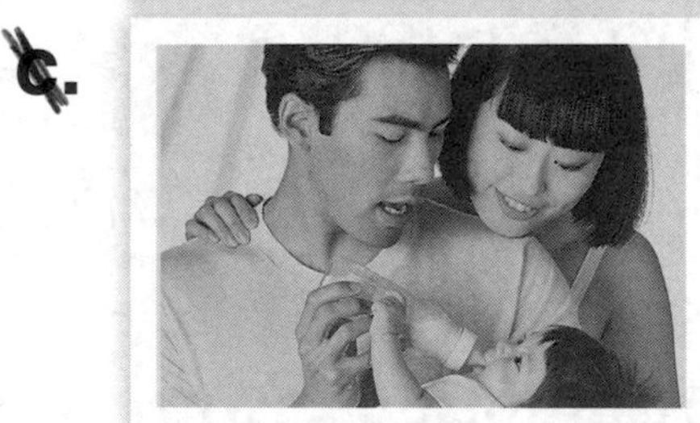

d. 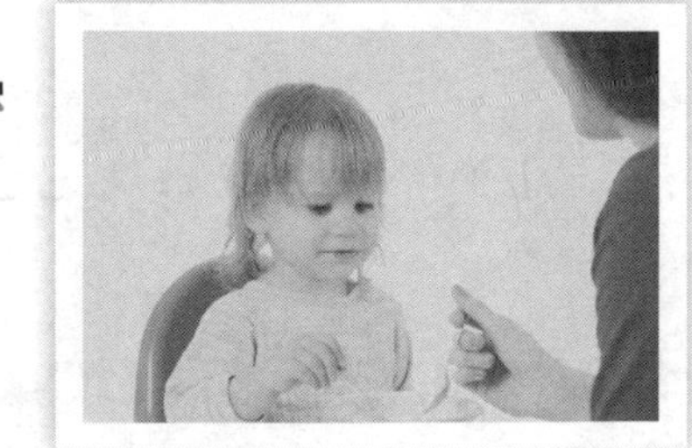

Name ______________________ Date __________

Grammar: Simple Present

Use the **simple present** to talk about things that happen all of the time.

Circle the correct word that completes each sentence.

Example: (Do, Does) your sister play soccer?

1. (Do, Does) you have brown hair?
   No, I (do not, does not).
2. (Do, Does) your friend like to swim?
   Yes, she (do, does).
3. (Do, Does) your brothers play basketball?
   No, they (don't, doesn't).
4. (Do, Does) you have a backpack?
   Yes, I (do, does).

Writing

Read the sentences. Circle the error in each one. Write the correct sentences.

My dad get up early on Saturday.

mrdadgets up earlr on saturdar.

He make pancakes.

Hemakes Pancakes.

We likes to go to the park.

welike to go to the park

We takes our dog.

wetakeour dog

Name ______________________ Date __________

Vocabulary

A. Fill in the missing letters to complete the word.

Sight Words
yellow
five
does
own

Story Words
house
apartment
trailer

1. o w ____
2. t r ____ ____ l e r
3. a p a r t ____ ____ ____ ____
4. d o ____ s
5. h o u ____ ____
6. f i ____ e
7. y e ____ ____ o w

B. Write the word that completes each sentence.

8. Do you have your ______________ computer?
9. There are ______________ people in my family.
10. Mei has a ______________ backpack.

Phonics

A. Circle the word with the short *i* sound.

1. pin kite
2. pine wig
3. bit bite
4. fish fine

B. Draw a line to the word that names the picture.

5.  lips
6.  kick
7.  dig
8.  ill

Name ____________________ Date __________

Think It Over

Reread to tell about the story.

Jen and Jim live in an apartment in town. It has steps.

Jen wants a big pet, but the pet will not fit. Jim wants a fish.

A. Answer the questions.

1. Where is Jen and Jim's apartment?

   The apartment is in ______________.

2. What does the apartment have?

   It has ______________.

3. What does Jen want?

   Jen wants a ______________.

4. What does Jim want?

   Jim wants a ______________.

B. Fill in the diagram. Compare and contrast your home and Jen and Jim's home. Put things that are the same in the middle. Put things that are different on one side or the other.

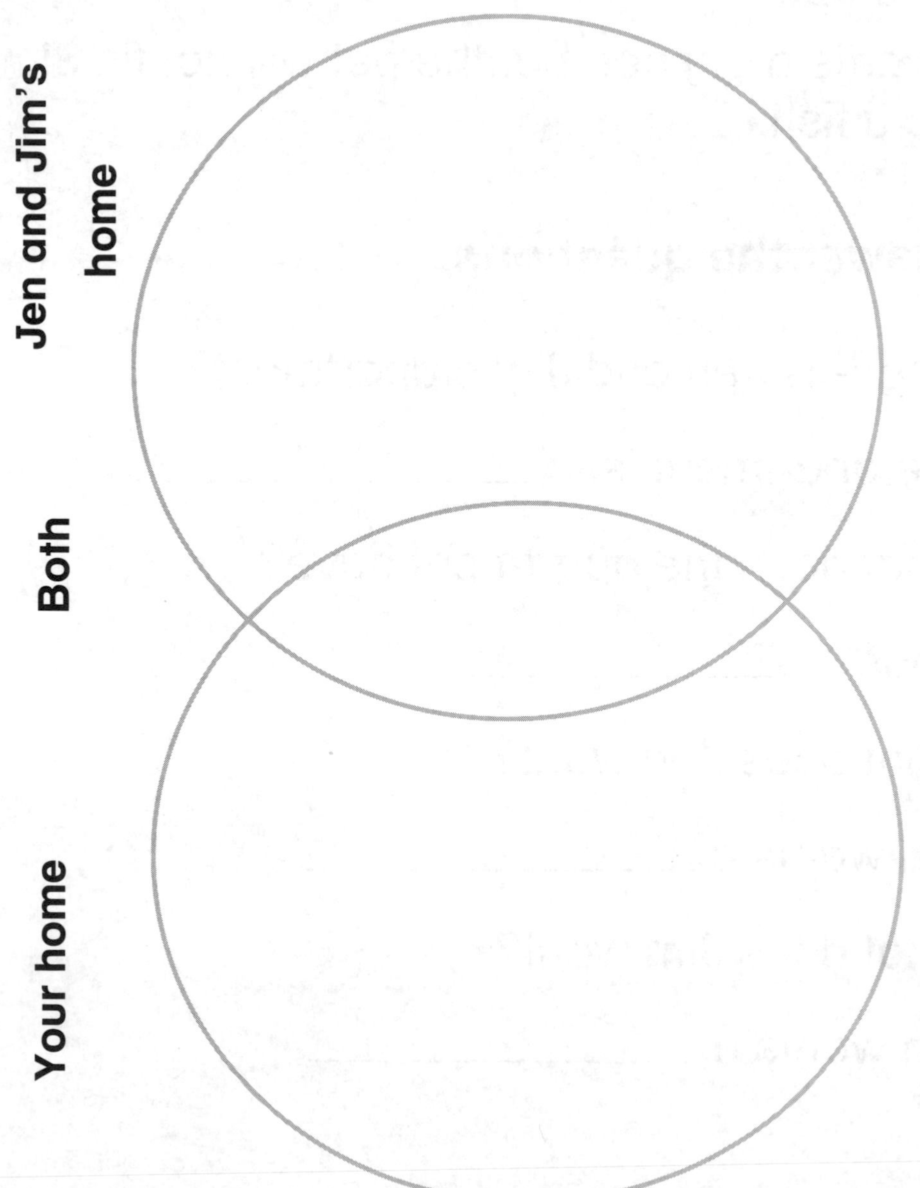

Name ______________________ Date __________

Grammar: *Be* Verbs

These are the simple present forms of the verb *be*: *am, is,* and *are*. The *be* verb must agree with the person, place, or thing you are talking about.

Choose a word from the box. Complete the sentence.

Example: She is my cousin.

am	is	are

1. We ______________ at school.

2. I ______________ happy today.

3. Who ______________ your teacher?

4. The dogs ______________ big.

5. The girl ______________ friendly.

Writing

Read the paragraph. Circle the five words that should begin with a capital letter. Write the words in the list.

My cousin rosa is fun. she likes to sing. we listen to music on saturday. We also like to dance. My friend marie likes to dance with us, too.

Words with Capital Letters

1. ______________
2. ______________
3. ______________
4. ______________
5. ______________

Name ______________________ Date __________

Review

Answer the questions after reading Unit 1. You can go back and reread to help find the answers.

1. Circle all the words with the short *a* sound.

Dan can grab a bag. Gramps can buy a ham.

2. In *Children Can Learn*, what happens because Nell is small? Circle the letter of the correct answer.

   a. She makes a mess.
   b. She takes a nap.
   c. She can get milk.
   d. She gets help from Mom.

3. Circle all the words with the short *e* sound.

Dad can help Bess. Bess can get milk.

4. Fill in the Word Web with names of family members.

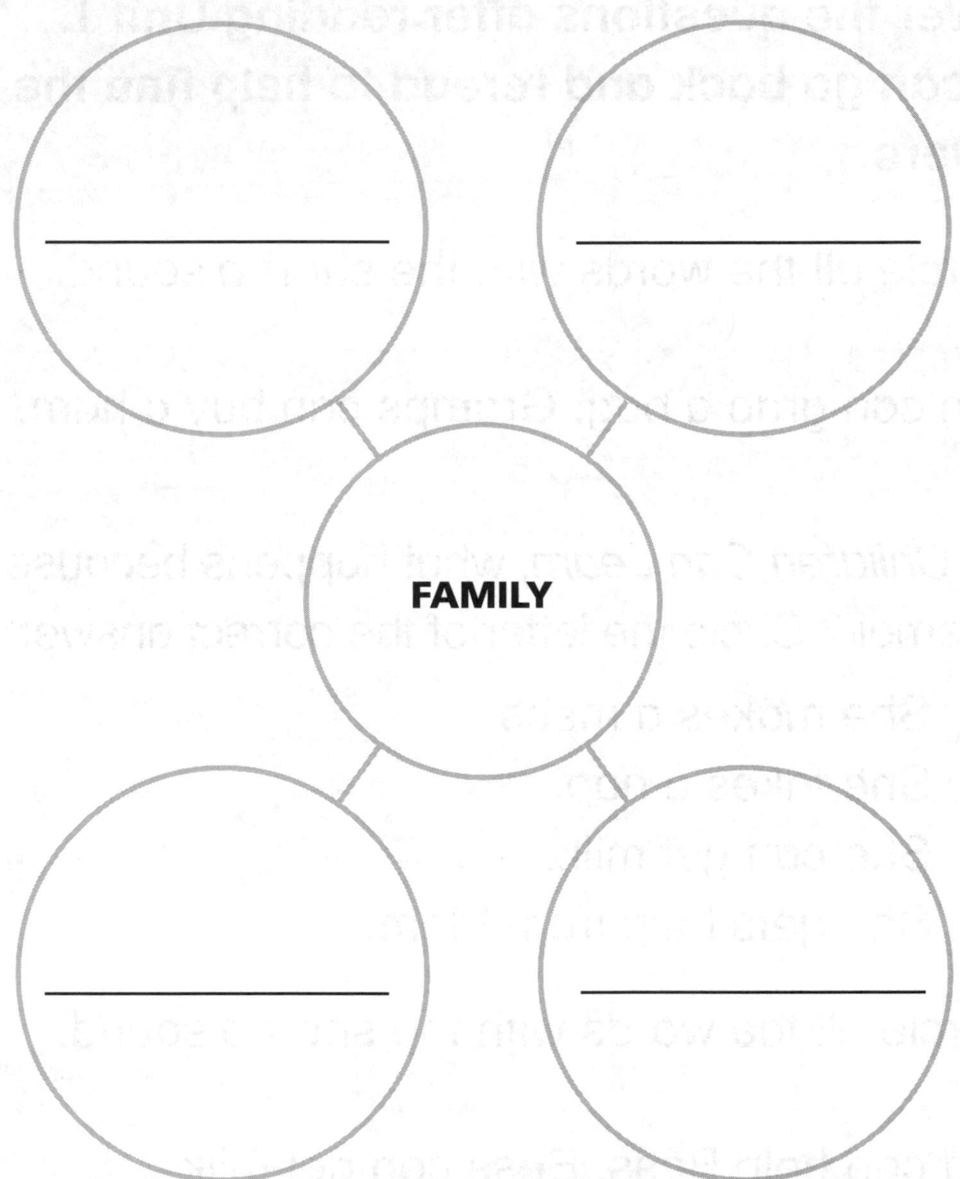

5. Circle all the words with the short *i* sound.

Jen wants a big pet, but it will not fit.

Name ______________________ Date __________

Writing Workshop: Write a Letter

Write a letter to a friend. Tell him or her what your home is like.

1. **Prewrite** Make a plan for your letter. List your ideas in the graphic organizer below.

Date ______________

Dear ______________________________

1. ______________________________

2. ______________________________

3. ______________________________

Your friend, ______

2. **Draft** Use your plan to write a letter.

3. **Revise** Read your letter. Do the sentences tell about your home? Try to write better sentences.

4. **Edit** Use the Editing Checklist on page 58 of your book to check your work. Correct your writing.

5. **Publish** Make a clean copy of your letter on a separate sheet of paper. Share it with the class.

Name ______________________ Date __________

Fluency

A. Take turns reading the sentences aloud with a partner. Use your finger to follow the words.

My apple is in the black bag.

There is a pen on the desk.

I think my pet fish is sick.

B. Read the sentences in Part A again. Choose one of the sentences. Draw a picture.

C. Take turns reading the sentences aloud with a partner. Use your finger to follow the words. Read aloud for one minute. Count your words.

Children Can Learn tells about	5
parents and how they help their	11
children learn new things. Moms and	17
Dads help feed their babies. They	23
help their children learn to spell	29
and to study for a math test. They	37
help their children with their bikes,	43
and with a bat and ball.	49

D. Read to your teacher, friends, or family.

Name ______________________________ Date ____________

Learning Checklist

Word Study and Phonics

- ☐ Two Syllable Words
- ☐ Short *a*; Consonants
- ☐ Short *e*; *th*
- ☐ Short *i*; *sh*

Reading Strategies

- ☐ Find the Main Idea
- ☐ Cause and Effect
- ☐ Predict

Grammar

- ☐ *Can* + Verb
- ☐ Simple Present
- ☐ *Be* Verbs

Writing

- ☐ Write about what you *can* and *can't* do.
- ☐ Write about a friend or a family member.
- ☐ Write about the picture of your family.
- ☐ Writing Workshop: Write a Letter

Listening and Speaking

- ☐ Story

Name ______________________ Date __________

Vocabulary

A. Fill in the missing letters. Then write the word.

Sight Words

light
hold
him
funny

1. li __ h __ ______________
2. f __ nn __ ______________
3. h __ ld ______________
4. hi __ ______________

Story Words

year
puppy
grown-up

B. Write the word that completes each sentence.

5. I am in second grade this ______________ .
6. In 15 years I will be a ______________ .
7. Can you ______________ my hand?
8. My ______________ is brown.

Phonics

A. Draw a line to the word that names the picture.

1.  fox

2.  socks

3.  pot

B. Complete each word with *o* or *wh*.

1. b ____ x	5. ____ x
2. cl ____ ck	6. h ____ p
3. ____ at	7. ____ ip
4. ____ ale	8. ____ eel

Name ____________________ Date __________

Think It Over

Reread to tell about the story.

Spot and I are big, and I am six. Now I cannot hold Spot. Spot and I play and learn tricks. Spot is a grown-up dog. I am still a kid.

A. Answer the questions.

1. Who tells the story?

   a. Spot
   b. the boy
   c. a grown-up
   d. the girl

2. What do Spot and the boy do?

   ____

3. Who is grown-up now? Circle the letter of the correct answer.

   a. Spot
   b. the baby
   c. the girl
   d. the boy

B. Write a character's name from *Spot Is a Pal* in the top circle. Then write two traits that the character has in the other circles. Give an example of the trait from the text.

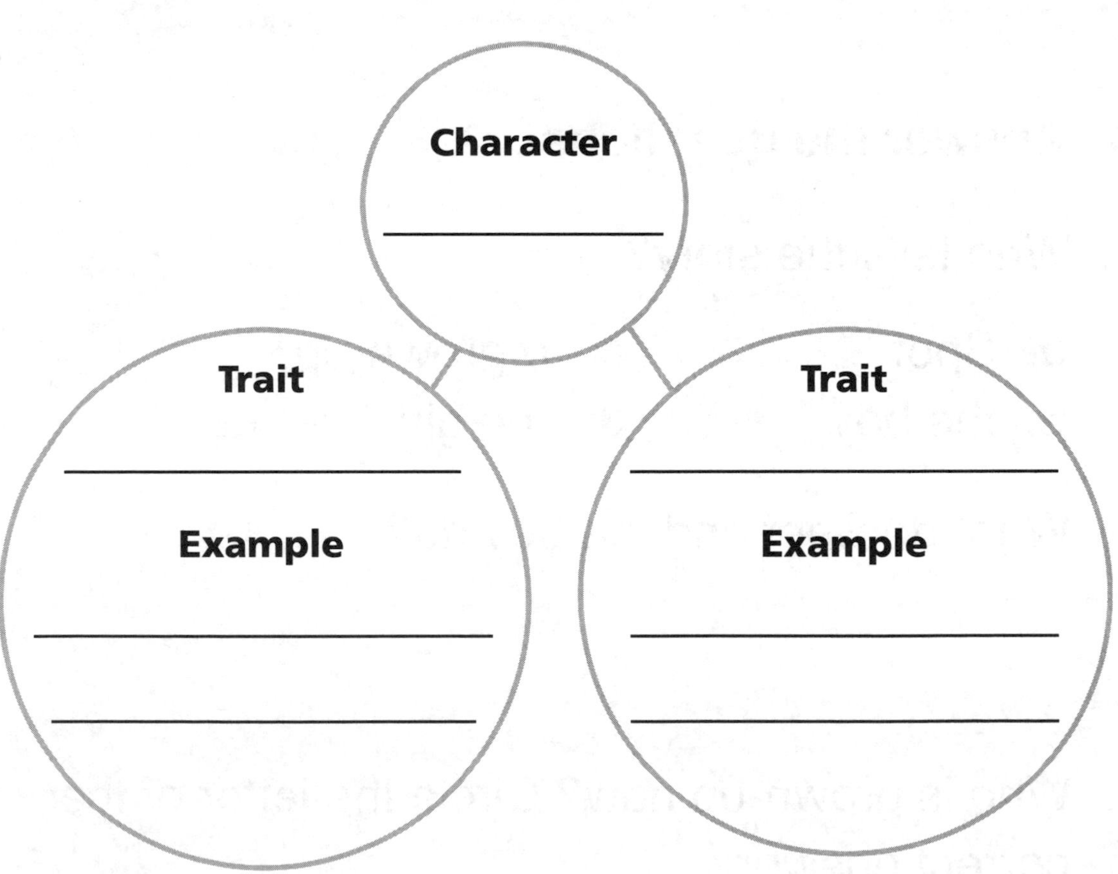

Name ______________________ Date __________

Grammar: More Simple Present

Use the **simple present** to talk about things that happen all the time.

Write the word that completes the sentence. Use the simple present.

Example: (help) Mom helps me bake cookies.

1. (work) Dad ______________ on the computer.
2. (play) We ______________ after school.
3. (teach) Mr. Simm ______________ us to read.
4. (run) Mom ______________ after work.
5. (live) They ______________ in an apartment.
6. (read) I ______________ books at school and at home.

Writing

Read the sentences. Circle the error in each one. Write the correct sentences.

I likes to make cookies.

First, I mixes flour and sugar.

Next, I puts in oil and eggs.

Then I bakes the cookies.

Name ______________________ Date __________

Vocabulary

Sight Words

her
cry
left
away

Story Words

people
beautiful
swan

A. Write the word that completes each sentence.

1. I can hear the baby ____________.
2. My dog ran ____________. I am sad.
3. The mother fed ____________ baby.
4. We have one class ____________ today.

B. Circle six vocabulary words in the Word Search.

A	C	R	Y	E	M	L	P	B	T	N	C	R	Y	E
P	C	F	U	S	W	A	N	O	A	E	P	S	Y	Y
A	W	A	Y	Z	M	L	P	C	A	L	S	W	A	N
B	E	A	U	T	I	F	U	L	P	E	O	P	L	E
M	C	L	R	E	H	L	P	O	E	F	A	W	A	Y
O	P	E	O	P	L	E	P	A	H	T	H	E	R	O

Phonics

A. Complete each word with the letter *u*. Say the word. Draw a line to its picture.

1. j ____ g

2. n ____ t

3. b ____ g

4. r ____ g

5. tr ____ ck

B. Complete each word with the letters *ch*. Draw a line to its picture.

6. lun ____

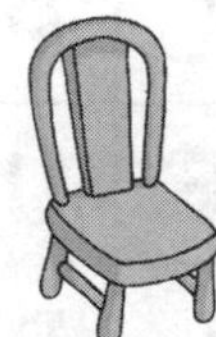

7. ____ air

Name ______________________ Date __________

Think It Over

Reread to tell about the story.

He is not a duckling. He is a swan! Other swans are his friends. People watch him swim and children throw bread to him. He hears them say, "The new swan is the most beautiful of all." At last he belongs.

A. Answer the questions.

1. What is the duckling now? Circle the letter of the correct answer.

   a. a duck **c.** a swan

   b. a man **d.** a child

2. What do people say about him?

   ____

3. How does he feel at the end of the story? Circle the letter of the correct answer.

   a. sad **c.** thin

   b. ugly **d.** glad

B. Write sentences to tell what happens to the ugly duckling at the beginning, middle, and end of the story.

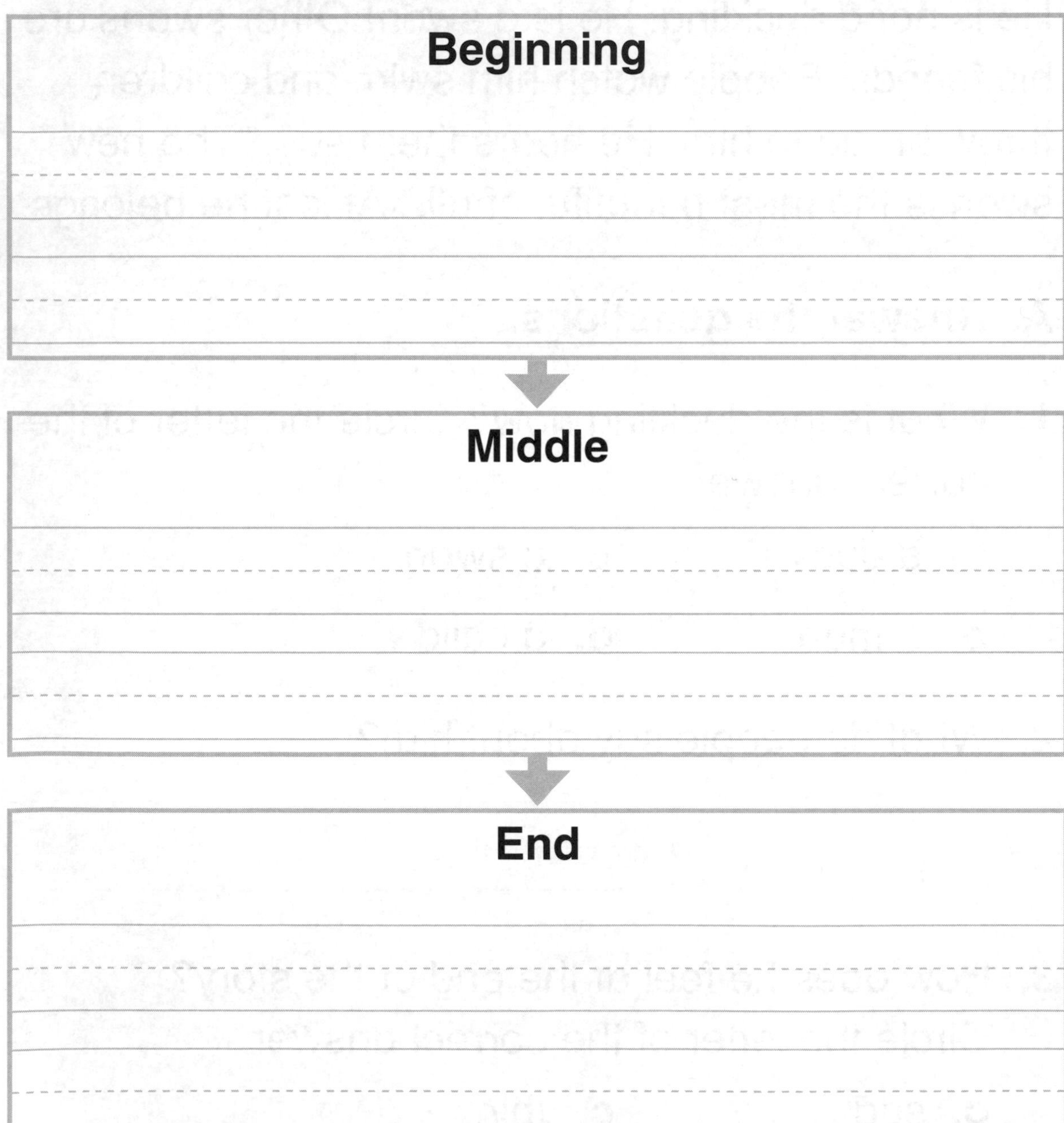

Name ______________________ Date __________

Grammar: Subject and Object Pronouns

A pronoun stands for a noun.

Choose the correct word from the box to replace the underlined word. Rewrite the sentence.

Example: Mrs. Allan works at the store.
She works at the store.

She	He	They

her	them

1. Dad likes to sing.

____

2. Jim and Maria draw pictures.

____

3. Grandmother reads to my brother.

____

4. My dog likes bones.

____

5. I play with my sister.

____

Writing

Read the sentences. Circle the error in each one. Write the correct sentences.

Baby chicks are little. It are fuzzy.

Grandpa feed the chicks.

He gives it water.

The chicks grows.

Name ____________________ Date __________

Vocabulary

Sight Words
- stay
- things
- place
- idea

Story Words
- heat
- pool
- cool

A. Write the letters in the right order to make a word.

1. h t e a ____________
2. p l c a e ____________
3. o o l c ____________
4. y a t s ____________
5. o p o l ____________

B. Write the word that completes each sentence.

6. Let's meet at Karen's ____________.
7. This ____________ makes me hot and tired.
8. Do you want to swim at the ____________?
9. It is ____________ at the park under the trees.
10. I have a good ____________. Listen.

Phonics

A. Complete the word.

1. c __ k __

2. l __ k __

3. sn __ k __

4. pl __ t __

B. Circle the word with the long *a* sound.

5. lamp lake
6. snake snap
7. plane plan
8. gas gate
9. rake rat
10. ant ate

Name ____________________ Date __________

Think It Over

Reread to tell about the story.

Mom: It will be too hot to go outside today. We will have to stay in. We will find things to do at home.

Rosa: I do not want to stay home another day! I want to get out of the house.

A. Answer the questions. Complete each sentence.

1. What will it be like outside?

   It will be very ____________________.

2. Where does Mom want to stay?

   Mom wants to stay ____________________.

3. What does Rosa want to do?

   Rosa wants to ____________________.

B. Read each problem in the chart below. In the next column, write the solution to the problem.

Problem	Solution
1. It is too hot to go outside.	
2. Rosa and Joe do not want to stay home.	

Name ______________________ Date __________

Grammar: *Will* + Verb

Use ***will* + verb** to talk about things in the future.

Write *will* or *won't* to complete each sentence.

Example: Will you eat a snack? Yes, I will.

1. ______________ you go to the playground?

   Yes, I ______________.

2. ______________ she play at the beach?

   No, she ______________.

3. ______________ her cousin swim?

   Yes, he ______________.

4. ______________ it rain today?

   No, it ______________.

5. ______________ they ride their bikes?

   Yes, they ______________.

Writing

Read the paragraph. Circle the six words that should begin with a capital letter. Write the words in the list.

i will do my homework after school. then Mom and I will go to the store. we will shop for dinner. before we go home, we'll visit aunt jane.

Words with Capital Letters

1. ________________
2. ________________
3. ________________
4. ________________
5. ________________
6. ________________

Name ____________________ Date __________

Review

Answer the questions after reading Unit 2. You can go back and reread to help find the answers.

1. Circle all the words with the short *o* sound. Underline the words with the *wh* sound.

I was five when I got Spot.

2. What happens to Spot in the story?

3. In *The Ugly Duckling*, who tells the duckling, "Go away!"? Circle the letter of the correct answer.

   a. his sisters
   b. Mama Duck
   c. the other swans
   d. the frog

4. Why do you think people watch him swim at the end of the story?

5. Circle all the words with the short *u* sound. Underline the words with the *ch* sound.

We have a chore. We must clean up the house.

6. What problem do Rosa and Joe have in *Fun on a Hot Day*? Circle the letter of the correct answer.

   a. They have to stay inside because of the cold weather.

   b. They have to stay inside because of the hot weather.

   c. They do not like the cold weather.

   d. They have to stay inside because of the rain.

7 . How do Rosa and Joe solve their problem?

Name ______________________ Date ________

Writing Workshop: Write to Compare and Contrast

Compare and contrast two sports or games.

1. **Prewrite** Choose two sports or games to compare. List your ideas in the graphic organizer below.

______________ **Both** ______________

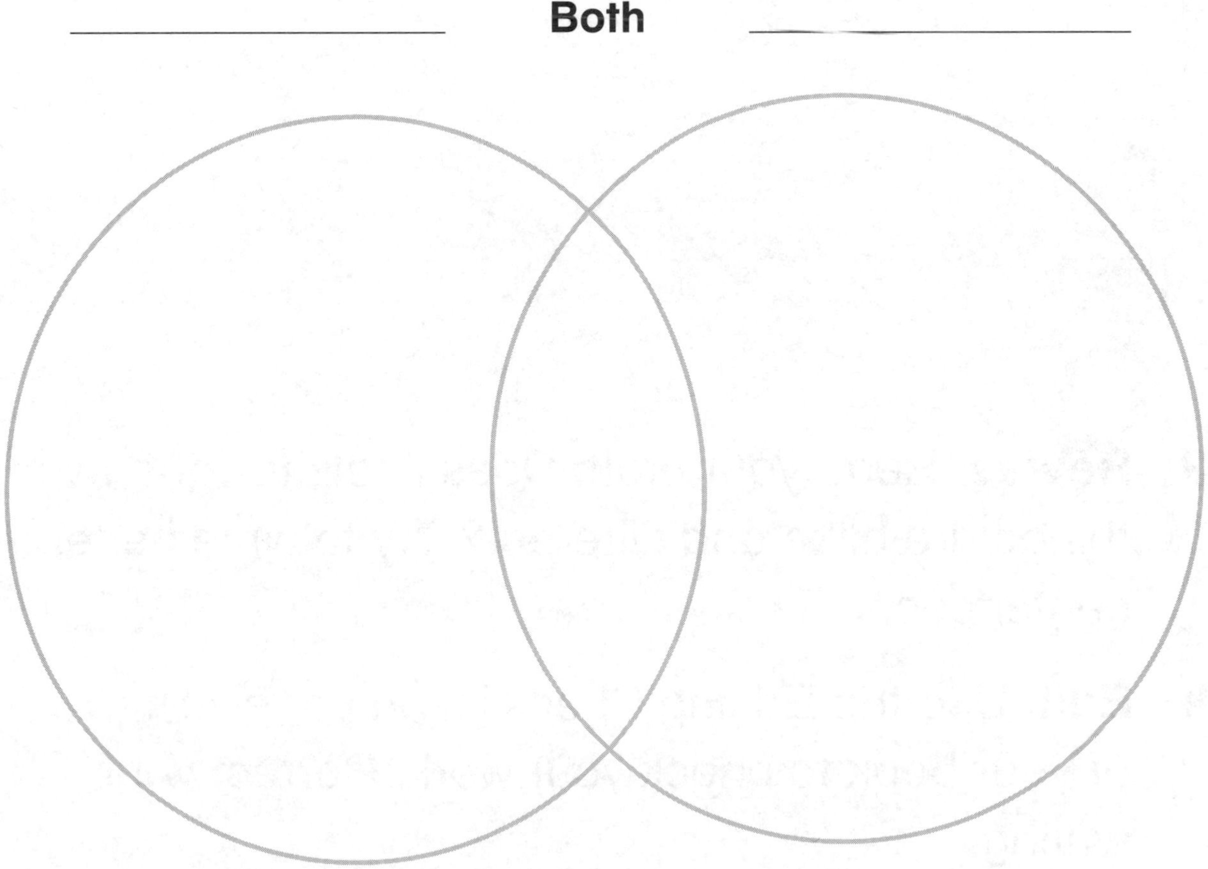

2. **Draft** Use your ideas to write a first draft.

3. **Revise** Read your draft. Does it tell how the two things are alike and different? Try to write better sentences.

4. **Edit** Use the Editing Checklist on page 114 of your book to check your work. Correct your writing.

5. **Publish** Make a clean copy of your final draft on a sheet of paper. Share it with the class.

Name ______________________ Date __________

Fluency

A. Take turns reading the sentences aloud with a partner. Use your finger to follow the words.

The water in the teapot is hot.

I forgot my lunch on the bus.

Ann ate the whole plate of cake.

B. Read the sentences in Part A again. Choose one of the sentences. Draw a picture.

C. Take turns reading the sentences. Use your finger to follow the words. Read aloud for one minute. Count your words.

The Ugly Duckling tells about a mother duck and her baby 11
ducks. One duckling came from a big egg. All the other 22
baby ducks see he is not like them. They say he is ugly. 35
Duck is sad. No one plays with him. Time passes. He is a 48
beautiful swan. 50

D. Read to your teacher, friends, or family.

Name ______________________ Date __________

Learning Checklist

Word Study and Phonics

- ☐ Compound Words
- ☐ Short *o: wh*
- ☐ Short *u: ch*
- ☐ Long *a*

Reading Strategies

- ☐ Identify Characters
- ☐ Make Inferences
- ☐ Problem and Solution

Grammar

- ☐ More Simple Present
- ☐ Subject and Object Pronouns
- ☐ *Will* + Verb

Writing

- ☐ Tell about a friend.
- ☐ Tell about an animal.
- ☐ Tell about what you will do on the weekend.
- ☐ Writing Workshop: Write to Compare and Contrast

Listening and Speaking

- ☐ Interview

Name ____________________ Date __________

Vocabulary

A. Write the word that completes each sentence.

Sight Words

special
day
laugh
family

Story Words

beach
baseball
tree

1. I love my grandma. She is a very ______________ person.
2. What ______________ is there no school?
3. I like to ______________ with my friends.
4. My ______________ has dinner together.

B. Fill in the missing letters to complete the word.

5. base ______
6. bea ______
7. ______ ee
8. f ______ ily
9. ______ ecial
10. la ______

Phonics

A. Write the word that names the picture.

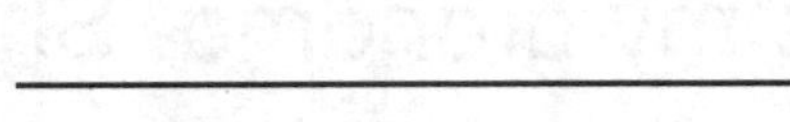

3. 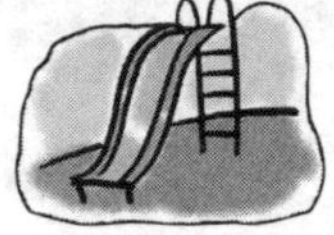 ____________________

4.  ____________________

B. Circle the word with the long *i* sound.

5. Mike men

6. kite kit

7. dinner dime

8. pin pine

9. ripe rip

10. time Tim

Name ______________________ Date __________

Think It Over

Reread to tell about the story.

Sam's dad takes him to a baseball game. The game is a special time. They sit in the red seats. Dad and Sam can see it all from there! Sam and his dad eat snacks. Sam jumps up to get a ball. It is a special time.

A. Answer the questions.

1. Who goes to a baseball game?

2. What can they see from the red seats?

3. Why do you think this is a special time for Sam and his dad?

B. Read the words in the center circle. Think of what families do together and fill in the other circles.

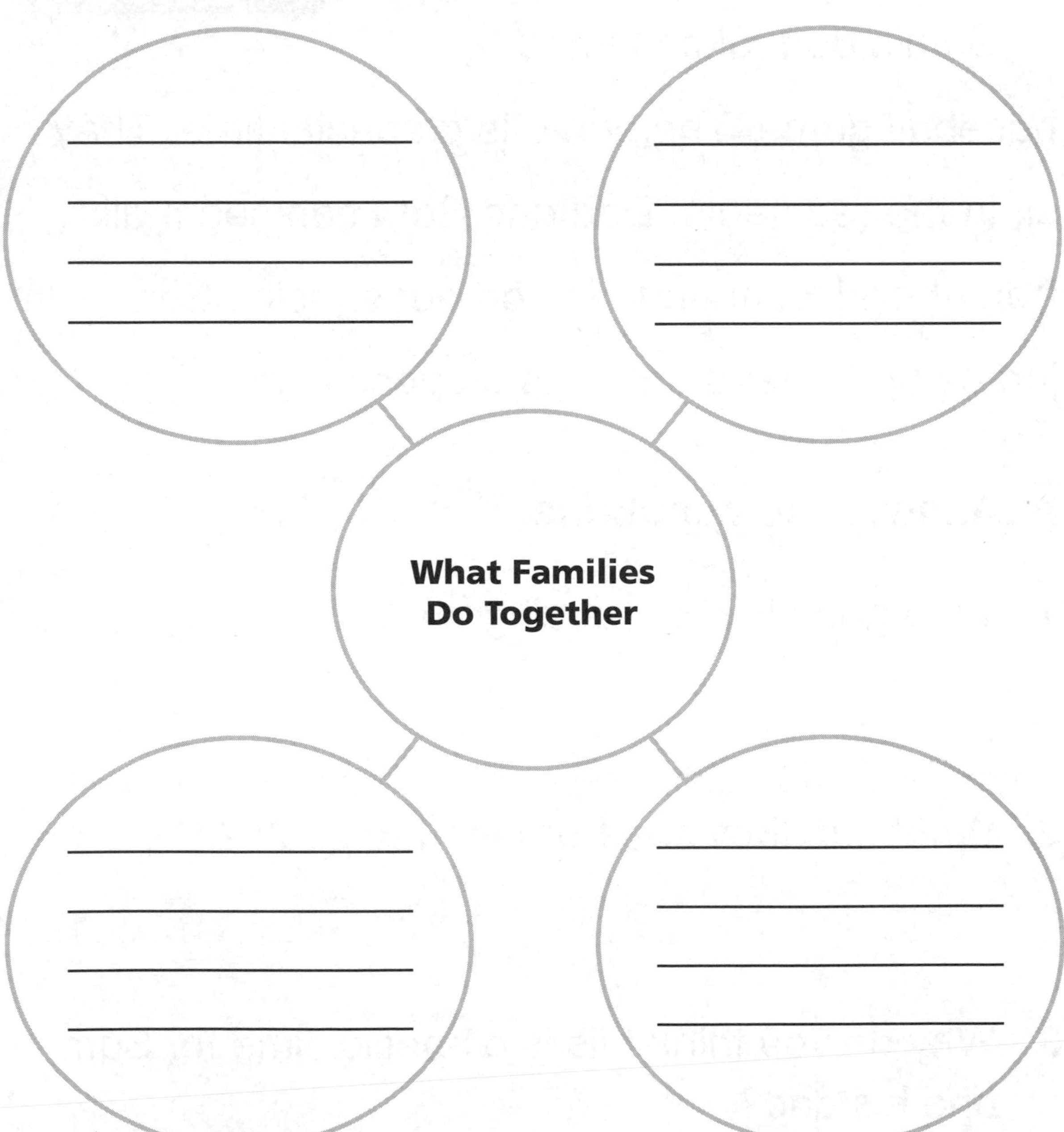

Name ______________________ Date __________

Grammar: Nouns

A **noun** names a person, place, or thing. Use **a** or **an** to talk about one noun. Add ***-s*** or ***-es*** to talk about two or more nouns.

Circle the correct word. Write it in the sentence.

Example: I have five (present, presents).

1. We ate a birthday (cake, cakes).
2. I am going to a (party, parties).
3. Dan will sing three (song, songs).
4. Five (friend, friends) are on the team.
5. Many (dog, dogs) are at the park.
6. The two (family, families) live on my street.
7. The (beach, beaches) are beautiful.
8. I have an (apple, apples) in my lunch bag.

Writing

Read the paragraph. Circle the five incorrect nouns. Write the correct noun in the list below.

Bill has a parties on his birthday. Many friend come to the party. His friends give him many present. He has a birthday cakes, too. Bill's friends play two or three game at the party.

Correct Nouns

1. ____________________
2. ____________________
3. ____________________
4. ____________________
5. ____________________

Name ____________________ Date __________

Vocabulary

A. Write the word that completes each sentence.

Sight Words
who
some
cold
keep

Story Words
roost
beehive
horse

1. Eat ______________ lunch before you go outside.
2. It's a very ______________ day! Please wear a hat.
3. I will give my sister the red balloon. I will ______________ the blue balloon.
4. ______________ wants to see a honey bee?
5. Jan can ride a ______________ .

B. Fill in the missing letters. Then write the word.

6. r ____ st ______________
7. hor ____ ______________
8. beehi ____ ______________

Phonics

A. Write the word that names the picture.

1.  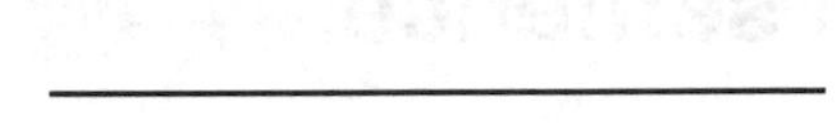

2.  

3.  

4. 

B. Circle the word with the long *o* sound.

5. robe rob
6. globe glob
7. bone bond
8. cane cone
9. hose hot
10. poke plop
11. hop hope
12. home hog

Name ______________________ Date __________

Think It Over

Reread to tell about the story.

Who woke up? Joe woke up.

Joe is getting an egg from a hen.

The hens are roosting in nests. Joe is getting lots of eggs. He will keep some eggs, and he will sell some eggs.

A. Answer the questions.

1. What did Joe get from the hen?
   He got an ____________________ .
2. What does Joe do with the eggs?
   He will ____________________ .
3. Why do you think the hens roost in nests?
   Hens roost in nests because they
   ____________________ .

B. Read the sentences. Complete the chart for Kate, Jane, and Jan.

What They Like	Why They Like It
Joe likes to get up in the morning.	He likes to gather eggs from his hens.
Kate likes to check on her beehives.	She __________.
Jane likes to milk her cow, Bell.	She __________.
Jan likes her horse, Rose.	She __________.

Name ______________________ Date __________

Grammar: Present Progressive

Use the **present progressive** to talk about things that are happening now.

A. Use *am*, *is*, or *are* to complete each sentence. Write the word.

Example: I am getting a snack.

1. My sister __________ baking cookies.
2. They __________ sitting.
3. Mom and Dad __________ listening.
4. I __________ having fun.
5. My friend __________ jumping rope.
6. Juan __________ walking the dog.
7. I __________ reading a book.
8. We __________ watching TV.
9. He __________ talking to his dad.

Writing

The paragraph below is missing six periods. Write the periods at the end of each sentence.

I am watching my dog He is running He is walking Now he is barking My dog is tired He wants some water

Name ______________________ Date __________

Vocabulary

A. Circle five vocabulary words in the Word Search.

S	W	E	D	R	M
D	J	F	O	M	I
O	B	A	W	H	D
N	K	O	N	E	D
E	P	S	H	U	L
S	B	A	L	L	E

Sight Words

we

done

ball

down

Story Words

kick

soccer

middle

B. Write the word or words that complete each sentence.

8. Let's sit __________ when we are __________.

9. Paco can __________ the __________.

10. Stand in the __________________ of the circle.

11. Now __________ are listening to music.

12. Do you like to play __________________?

Phonics

A. Circle the word with the long *u* sound.

1. cute cut
2. June gum
3. cub cube
4. use under
5. uncle uniform

B. Draw a line to the word that names the picture.

5.  cube
6.  mule
7. 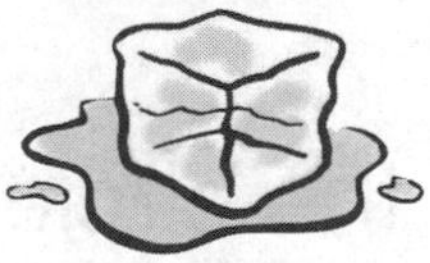 use

Name ______________________ Date __________

Think It Over

Reread to tell about the story.

County Fairs
Occur in June
They are great fun
But end too soon.

Go on rides
Eat treats by the heap
Then say good-bye
To get some sleep.

A. Answer the questions.

1. What happens in June?

____

2. What do people eat at the County Fair?

____

3. Why do you think the author says County Fairs end too soon?

____

B. Look at the pictures. Fill in the chart with words that name fun things to do.

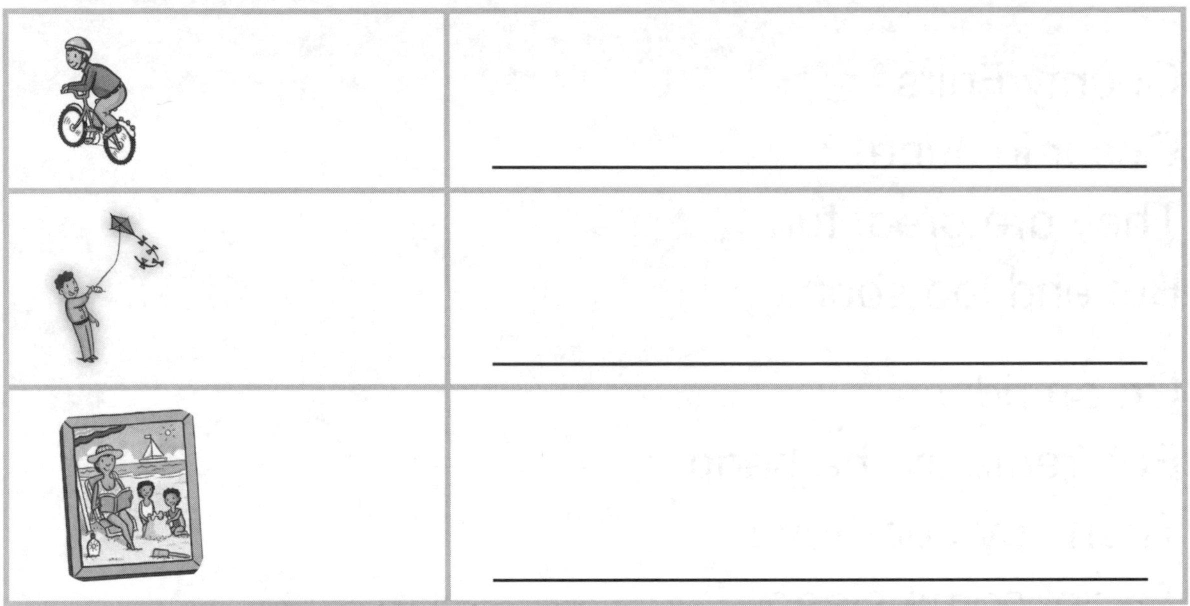

Draw a picture of something you would like to do and play.

Name ______________________ Date __________

Grammar: Adjectives

Adjectives describe nouns. They can go before a noun. An adjective can also follow *be*.

Choose an adjective from the box to complete each sentence. Use each word once. Underline the noun that the adjective describes.

Example: Ava has long hair.

soft
tall
fun
cold
little
black

1. Sam has ______________ hair.
2. The water is ______________.
3. I have a ______________ sister. She is two.
4. This is a ______________ game. I like it.
5. These socks are ______________. They feel nice.
6. That building is ______________.

Writing

Read the sentences. Circle the error in each one. Write the correct sentences.

I have hair black.

My sister, gina, has brown hair.

We have are brown eyes.

Our brother has brown hair and green eyes

Name ______________________ Date __________

Review

Answer the questions after reading Unit 3. You can go back and reread to help find the answers.

1. Circle all the words with the long *i* sound.

It is time to fly my kite. I will have a good time.

2. In *A Special Time*, what do Sam and his dad do at the baseball game?

3. Who likes to hike?

______________________ like to hike.

4. In *Who Woke Up?*, why do you think Joe keeps some eggs?

5. Circle all the words with the long *o* sound.

We pet Rose on her soft nose.

6. Circle all the words with the long *u* sound.

They use mules to help them work.

7. In *Playing Games*, what activity does the author NOT talk about? Circle the letter of the correct answer.

a. playing soccer

b. playing golf

c. riding horses

d. jumping in hay

8. What do you like to do with your friends, family, or on your own? Write two or three sentences.

Name ______________________ Date __________

Writing Workshop: Write a Descriptive Paragraph

You will write a paragraph describing a holiday.

1. **Prewrite** Choose a holiday to describe. List your ideas in the graphic organizer below.

I see	I hear	I taste

____

2. **Draft** Use your ideas to write a first draft.

3. **Revise** Read your draft. Do the sentences describe the holiday? Try to write better sentences.

4. **Edit** Use the Editing Checklist on page 174 of your book to check your work. Correct your writing.

5. **Publish** Make a clean copy of your final draft on a sheet of paper. Share it with the class.

Name ______________________ Date __________

Fluency

A. Take turns reading the sentences aloud with a partner. Use your finger to follow the words.

It's time to play on the slide!

My dog dug a hole for his bone.

Do you like to play music?

B. Read the sentences in Part A again. Choose one of the sentences. Draw a picture.

Fluency

C. Take turns reading the sentences. Use your finger to follow the words. Read aloud for one minute. Count your words.

Who Woke Up? tells about people	6
and the things they do in the morning.	14
Bob gets eggs. Mike and Jim eat eggs	22
and bread. Kate gets honey from bees.	29
Jane gets a pail of milk from Bell.	37
The cow eats hay. Jan rides her horse.	45
Children pet the horse. Kids laugh and	52
joke and have a good time.	58

D. Read to your teacher, friends, or family.

Name ______________________ Date __________

Learning Checklist

Word Study and Phonics

- ☐ Antonyms and Synonyms
- ☐ Long *i*
- ☐ Long *o*
- ☐ Long *u*

Reading Strategies

- ☐ Author's Purpose
- ☐ Find Details
- ☐ Use Prior Knowledge

Grammar

- ☐ Nouns
- ☐ Present Progressive
- ☐ Adjectives

Writing

- ☐ Describe what you do on your birthday.
- ☐ Describe what a classmate is doing.
- ☐ Describe an object.
- ☐ Writing Workshop: Write a Descriptive Paragraph

Listening and Speaking

- ☐ Description Game

Name ______________________ Date __________

Vocabulary

Sight Words
friends
roads
very
letter

Story Words
simple
e-mail
board

A. Write the word that completes each sentence.

1. A word that means "streets" is ______________ .
2. I invited my ______________ to a party.
3. That is a ______________ question. Even my little brother can answer it.
4. I like strawberries ______________ much.
5. I use the computer to write an ______________ to my grandma.

B. Write the letters in the correct order to make a word.

6. r e f i s d n ______________
7. r o b a d ______________
8. t e l e r t ______________

Phonics

A. Write *ai* or *ay* to complete each word.

1.  tr ____ n

2.  pl ____

3.  sn ____ l

4.  r ____ n

B. Write *th* or *ch* to complete each word.

5.  ____ ree

6.  pea ____

7.  ba ____

8. 

____ alk

Name ______________________ Date __________

Think It Over

Reread to tell about the story.

A long time ago, we drove on roads that had a lot of rocks and bumps. A horse led the way. We used a stick and a rope to tell the horse which way to go. We pulled the rope to say, "Stop!"

A. Answer the questions.

1. How were roads in the past?

2. How did the horse know which way to go?

3. Why do you think the roads were full of rocks and bumps?

B. Complete the KWL Chart. In the first column, write about how people lived long ago. Write what you want to know in the middle column. In the last column, write what you learned.

K- What I Know	W- What I Want to Know	L- What I Learned

Name ______________________ Date __________

Grammar: Simple Past Tense

Use the **past tense** to talk about events that happened in the past.

Add *-ed* to the main verb to form the past tense.

Choose a word from the box to complete the sentence. Write the past tense of the verb.

Example: Mom walked to the store.

1. Dad ______________ dinner last night.
2. We ______________ to music.
3. My friends ______________ soccer over the weekend.
4. Marcus ______________ at my joke.
5. I ______________ to read last year.

play
laugh
~~walk~~
cook
listen
learn

Writing

Read the sentences. Circle the error in each one. Write the correct sentences.

I e-mail my sister yesterday.

I want to tell her about my surprise.

Grandma mail me a card!

She does not forget my birthday.

Name ____________________ Date __________

Vocabulary

A. Write the word that matches the clue.

Sight Words
near
sure
good
other

Story Words
tasty
treat
waffle

1. opposite of bad ____________
2. not this one ____________
3. opposite of far ____________
4. you have no doubt ____________

B. Write the word that completes each sentence.

5. Ice cream is a special ____________ .
6. A ____________ cone holds a lot of ice cream.
7. Berries make a ____________ dessert.

Phonics

A. Circle the words with the long *e* sound.

Clean clothes feel soft and nice.

B. Draw a line to the word that names the picture.

1.  sleep
2.  read
3.  peach
4.  meat
5.  leaf

Name ______________________ Date __________

Think It Over

Reread to tell about the story.

A big fair was held in 1904. The sun was bright and high in the clear, blue sky. A lot of kids and adults came to play and have fun. They were hot. They ate a lot of ice cream.

A. Answer the questions.

1. Why were the people hot?

2. Why do you think people like to eat ice cream?

3. Draw a picture of a fair.

B. Write words that tell about ice cream.

Name ______________________ Date __________

Grammar: Past *Be*

Use the past tense of ***be*** to talk about the past.

Use ***was*** with *I, he, she,* and *it*.

Use ***were*** with *you, we,* and *they*.

Write *was* or *were* to complete the sentence.

Example: Our lunch was good.

1. The dog ______________ not hurt.
2. Mom and Dad ______________ happy.
3. The music ______________ not loud.
4. The pool water ______________ cold.
5. The cookies ______________ good.

Writing

Read the paragraph. It is missing five periods. Add the periods.

I was at the beach. My friend came with me
Mom stayed in the shade We played in the sand
Mom gave us ice cream We had lots of fun

Name ______________________ Date __________

Vocabulary

A. Write the letters in the correct order to make a word.

Sight Words

- lady
- wife
- began
- born

1. f w e i ________________
2. r o n b ________________
3. d y a l ________________
4. a g b e n ________________

Story Words

- flowers
- highway
- legacy

B. Draw a line to match each word with its clue.

5. highway — a. This is a road that connects towns.
6. legacy — b. These are parts of a plant.
7. flowers — c. This is something handed down to others.

Phonics

A. Circle the words with the long *i* or the soft *g* sound.

1. The lights are bright tonight.
2. Sam flies his kite at the beach.
3. I wrote nine sentences on the page.
4. My sister sang the song on a stage.
5. Jim has a very nice smile.

B. Complete the word that names the picture.

6.  n ____ t

7.  sl ____ de

8. 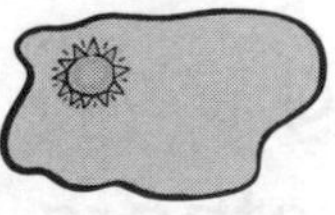 sk ____

9.  ____ ie

Name ______________________ Date __________

Think It Over

Reread to tell about the story.

Today, Lady Bird's legacy lives on. Flowers are still planted at the nation's capital. Highways around the country have flowers planted by them, too. Lady Bird worked hard to keep America beautiful.

A. Answer the questions.

1. Where are flowers planted today?

2. What did Lady Bird work hard to do?

B. Think about Lady Bird Johnson's life. Number the events from 1–4 to show the order that they happened.

1. ________________ Lady Bird married Lyndon B. Johnson.
2. ________________ Lady Bird was born in 1912.
3. ________________ Lady Bird Johnson started a project. She planted millions of flowers.
4. ________________ Lyndon B. Johnson became President of the United States.

Name ______________________ Date __________

Grammar: Past Tense: Irregular Verbs

For regular verbs, do not add *-ed* to form the past tense. You have to remember the past form.

Draw a line to connect the present tense verb and the past tense verb.

1. come	ate
2. eat	slept
3. go	came
4. sleep	sat
5. sit	went

6. Choose two verbs in the past tense. Write a sentence with each verb.

Writing

Read the paragraph. Circle the words that need capital letters. Write the words in the list.

our family lives on greenville. Mrs. bell lives next door. she is a good friend to our family. Mrs. Bell helps my mom. she likes to plant flowers. mrs. Bell also makes the best cookies!

Words That Need Capital Letters

1. Our
2. ______________
3. ______________
4. ______________
5. ______________
6. ______________

Name ______________________ Date __________

Review

Answer the questions after reading Unit 4. Go back and reread if you need help.

1. Circle all the words with the long *a* sound.

Then she put it in the mail. A letter may take days to get to a friend.

2. What couldn't be done in the past? Circle the letter of the correct answer.

a. play chess
b. travel to another city
c. send an e-mail
d. wash clothes

3. Circle all the words with the long *e* sound.

We eat ice cream when we go to the beach.

4. In *Ice Cream Cones,* what did the ice cream man run out of? Circle the letter of the correct answer.

a. dishes
b. cones
c. ice cream
d. spoons

5. Why do you think kids still eat ice cream today?

6. What did Lady Bird Johnson do as First Lady? Circle the letter of the correct answer.

   a. She planted flowers around the capital.

   b. She began a program to beautify highways.

   c. She hired her own press secretary.

   d. All of the above.

7. How did Lady Bird Johnson make our country more beautiful?

Writing Workshop:
Write a Story

Write a story about something that happened a long time ago. It can be a true story or one that you make up.

1. **Prewrite** Plan your story. Use the chart to help.

Who is in the story? Write the names of the characters.	**Where does it happen? Write the time and the place.**
What problem does the main character have?	**How is the problem solved?**

2. **Draft** Use your chart to write a first draft.

3. **Revise** Read your draft. Do the sentences tell about the story? Try to write better sentences.

4. **Edit** Use the Editing Checklist on page 232 of your book to check your work. Correct your writing.

5. **Publish** Make a clean copy of your story on a sheet of paper. Share it with the class.

Name ______________________ Date __________

Fluency

A. Take turns reading the sentences aloud with a partner. Use your finger to follow the words.

I got an e-mail from my sister today.

The last leaf fell from the tree.

I like to bake apple cake.

B. Read the sentences in Part A again. Choose one of the sentences. Draw a picture.

C. **Take turns reading the sentences aloud with a partner. Use your finger to follow the words. Read aloud for one minute. Count your words.**

D. **Read to your teacher, friends, or family.**

Ice Cream Cones tells how a tasty treat we 9
love to eat came to be. At a big fair on a hot 22
day in 1904, a man ran out of dishes to put 33
his scoops of ice cream in. He still had lots 43
of ice cream to sell. A waffle man helped 52
him make cone shapes for the ice cream. 60

Learning Checklist

Word Study and Phonics

- ☐ Multiple-Meaning Words
- ☐ Long *a: ch, th*
- ☐ Long *e*
- ☐ Long *i*: soft *g*

Reading Strategies

- ☐ Draw Conclusions
- ☐ Summarize
- ☐ Ask Questionsw

Grammar

- ☐ Simple Past Tense
- ☐ Past: *Be*
- ☐ Past: Irregular Verbs

Writing

- ☐ Write about your day.
- ☐ Tell about your weekend.
- ☐ Tell about the life of someone in your family.
- ☐ Writing Workshop: Write a Story

Listening and Speaking

- ☐ Skit

Name ______________________ Date __________

Vocabulary

A. Write the word that completes each sentence.

Sight Words
have
small
found

Story Words
squirrel
nibbles
delicious

1. A ______________ runs across the yard.
2. She ______________ on a nut.
3. I ate a big ______________ apple for a snack.
4. I planted a ______________ tree with my dad.

B. Circle three vocabulary words in the Word Search.

S	U	L	Q	A	F
M	H	A	V	E	O
A	T	B	T	G	U
L	C	A	L	L	N
L	M	P	U	O	D

Phonics

A. Write the word that names the picture.

1.  ____________________

2.  ____________________

3. ____________________

4. 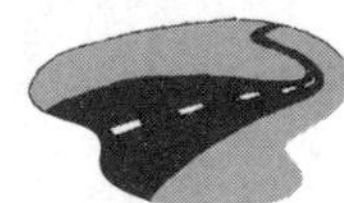 ____________________

B. Draw a line to the word that names the picture.

5.  stage

6.  blow

7. 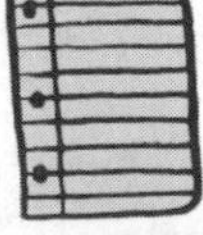 gem

8  page

Name ______________________ Date __________

Think It Over

Reread to tell about the story.

A nest with eggs sits high in this tree. Twigs, twine, and trash make up this nest. Mother bird will wait till her chicks grow in the eggs. Small chicks will poke holes and crack the shells. Then Mother will find a meal her chicks can eat.

A. Answer the questions.

1. What makes up the nest? Circle the answer.

   a. leaves **c.** feathers
   b. twigs, twine, and trash **d.** a tree

2. What is Mother bird waiting for?

   She is waiting for ______________________ .

3. How do the chicks get out of the eggs?

   The chicks __________________________ .

B. Read each sentence. Write the number of each Cause next to its Effect.

CAUSE	EFFECT
1. The bird sits on her eggs.	____ A fly gets stuck.
2. The spider spins a web.	____ It will have food for winter.
3. The bird catches a worm.	____ The chicks hatch.
4. The squirrel piles up nuts at home.	____ The chick can eat.

Name ______________________ Date __________

Grammar: Prepositions of Location

Some **prepositions** tell the location of places or things. They are called prepositions of location.

Choose one of the prepositions below. Use it to answer the question.

in on at next to under between

Example: Where is the cup? It is <u>in</u> the sink.

1. Where are your shoes?

   They are ________________ the bed.

2. Where on the stickers?

   They are ________________ the paper.

3. Where is the chair?

   It is________________ the table.

4. Where is your mom?

   She is ________________ the store.

Writing

Read the sentences. Circle the error in each one. Write the correct sentences.

I changed my bedroom on my house.

I put my bed under the dresser and the desk.

I put a poster at the wall.

I put my toys on a big box.

My desk between the bookcase.

Name ______________________ Date __________

Vocabulary

A. Write the word that completes each sentence.

Sight Words
was
said
soon
water

Story Words
arms
shore
sign

1. My dad ________________ he would arrive early.
2. I can reach the shelf when I stretch my ________________ up.
3. I like to play in the water by the ________________ .
4. It ________________ sunny when I got up.
5. ________________ is my favorite drink.

B. Circle the vocabulary words.

6. Mom lifted her arms out of the water.
7. The sign on the shore said, "Keep out of the water."

Phonics

A. Write the word that names the picture.

1.  ______________

2.  ______________

3.  ______________

4. 

____

B. Circle the words with the same sound as the *ue* in *clue*.

5. I ate fruit and soup.

6. I have a new blue coat.

7. We knew it was a true story.

8. Ed drew a picture of Sue.

Name ______________________ Date __________

Think It Over

Reread to tell about the story.

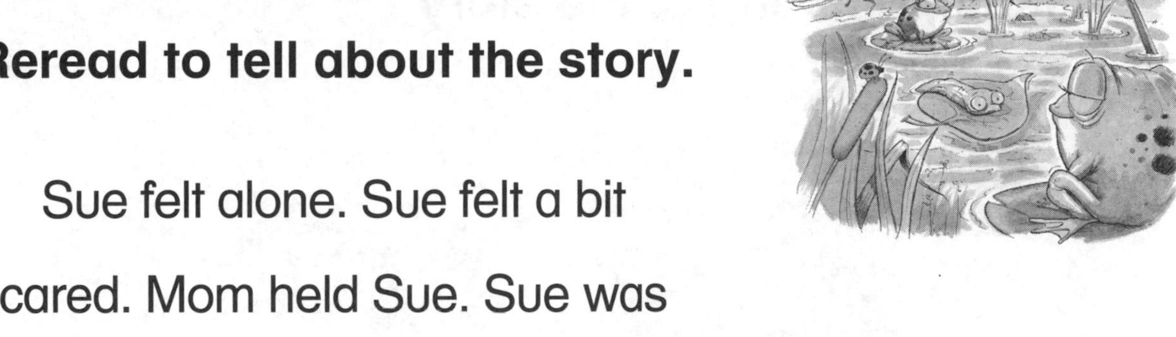

Sue felt alone. Sue felt a bit scared. Mom held Sue. Sue was cold and wet. She moaned, "Mom, when will I be a big frog?"

Mom said, "Soon. It is true. You will be a big frog in a few weeks."

A. Answer the questions.

1. Who is Sue?
   Sue is a ______________________.
2. How did she feel?
   Sue felt ______________________.
3. What was Sue's problem?
   Sue wanted ______________________.

B. Write what happened to Sue in the beginning, middle, and end of the story.

Beginning

Middle

End

Name ______________________ Date __________

Grammar: Adverbs of Manner

An **adverb** describes the action of a verb.
Add *-ly* to an adjective to make some adverbs.

Change the adjective to an adverb to complete each sentence.

Example: We talked quietly (quiet).

1. The team cheered ______________ (loud).
2. We cleaned up ______________ (quick).
3. Please write ______________ (neat).
4. The hikers walked ______________ (careful).
5. The birds sang ______________ (sweet).

Writing

Read the paragraph. It is missing four periods. Write periods where they belong.

The dog barked loudly. We looked outside No one was there. Our dog barked again I listened carefully The cat was outside. She was purring quietly

Name ______________________ Date __________

Vocabulary

A. Fill in the letter or letters to complete each word.

Sight Words

ground
air
more
animals

Story Words

ocelot
river
ecosystem

1. a i ____
2. r i ____ e ____
3. m ____ r ____
4. a n i ____ a ____ s
5. o c ____ l ____ t
6. g r ____ ____ n d
7. e ____ o s y s ____ e m

B. Write the word that completes each sentence.

8. We like to fish along the __________.
9. Many __________ live in the forest.
10. Let's find rocks on the __________.

Phonics

A. Circle the word with the same *ow* sound as in *clown*.

1. row gown
2. crowd throw
3. flower snow
4. cow blow

B. Write the word with *ou* that names the picture.

5.  ______________________

6.  ______________________

7.  ______________________

8.  ______________________

Name ______________________ Date __________

Think It Over

Reread to tell about the story.

The ocelot is about twice as big as a pet cat and has fur with lots of spots. The spots help the ocelot to hide so it can be safe and look for food. Ocelots come out at night.They may hunt birds, fish, and other small animals.

A. Answer the questions.

1. What does an ocelot look like?

____

2. How do spots help the ocelot?

____

3. What do ocelots hunt?

____

B. Complete the KWL Chart. In the first column, write what you already knew about plants and animals of the desert. In the middle column, write what you wanted to know. In the last column, write what you learned.

K- What I Know	W- What I Want to Know	L- What I Learned

Name ______________________ Date __________

Grammar: Possessives and Possessive Pronouns

The **possessive** form shows that someone owns something.
Add *'s* to a noun.
Add 'after the *s* for more than one noun.

Make the possessive form of the noun. Write the word in the sentence.

Example: (cousin) It is my <u>cousin's</u> book.

1. (friends) It is my ______________ team.
2. (dad) Here is ______________ car.
3. (dog) The ______________ collar is on the chair.
4. (students) The ______________ artwork was up on the wall.
5. (baby) The ______________ jacket is soft and warm.

Writing

Read the paragraph. Circle the words that need capital letters. Write the words in the list.

my brother mark has a new car. it is red. Mark's car has soft seats. the car has a CD player, too. Mark is a good driver. He took me for a ride on saturday.

1. My
2. ________________
3. ________________
4. ________________
5. ________________

Name ______________________ Date __________

Review

Answer the questions after reading Unit 5. You can go back and reread to help find the answers.

1. Circle all the words with the long *o* sound.

Some squirrels roam around and make homes in trees.

2. What does the spider eat? Circle the letter of the correct answer.

a. an egg **c.** an insect
b. a chick **d.** nuts

3. In *Sue the Tadpole*, what can Sue do at the beginning of the story? Circle the letter of the correct answer.

a. swim **c.** hop
b. jump **d.** run

4. In *Sue the Tadpole*, why does Sue say that it was worth waiting for arms and legs?

____

____

5. Circle the words with the same sound as the *ue* in *blue*.

Sue was sad. Mom said, "Soon. It is true. You will be a big frog in a few weeks."

6. Describe the ecosystem near the long river in the desert.

7. Circle the words with the same sound you hear in *clown.*

These big cats can hear a sound. Lions lie down all day.

8. Tell two things you learned in this unit.

Name ______________________________ Date ____________

Writing Workshop:

Write a Description

Write a description of a room.

1. **Prewrite** Plan your description. List your ideas in the chart below.

I see . . .	I hear . . .
I smell . . .	**I feel . . .**

2. **Draft** Use your chart to write a first draft.

3. **Revise** Read your draft. Can a reader picture what you describe? Try to write better sentences.

4. **Edit** Use the Editing Checklist on page 292 of your book to check your work. Correct your writing.

5. **Publish** Make a clean copy of your description on a sheet of paper. Share it with the class.

Fluency

A. Read the sentences aloud. Practice saying them as fast as you can with no mistakes.

1. George saw a goat
   eating rope on a boat.
2. The group got new spoons
   and soon ate all the soup.
3. The clown found a mouse
   in his big brown house.

B. Read each sentence several times. Then cover each one with your hand and try to say it word for word.

1. Birds make nests and spiders make webs in trees.
2. A fat little tadpole grows up to be a loud frog.
3. The desert ecosystem has very dry land.

C. Take turns reading the sentences aloud with a partner. Use your finger to follow the words. Read aloud for one minute. Count your words.

Sue the Tadpole tells the story of a	8
baby tadpole who wants to be a big frog	17
fast. She feels alone and scared. Her	24
mom and dad say she will grow in a few	34
weeks. Sue wants to jump and hop from	42
leaf to leaf in the pond right now. She	51
waits and waits. Time passes, and Sue	58
gets arms and legs. She gets a prize in	67
a jumping show.	70

D. Read to your teacher, friends, or family.

Learning Checklist

Word Study and Phonics

☐ Prefixes
☐ Long *o*: soft *g*
☐ Letters: *ew*, *ou*
☐ Letters: *ow, ou*

Reading Strategies

☐ Cause and Effect
☐ Sequence of Events
☐ Make Inferences

Grammar

☐ Prepositions of Location
☐ Adverbs of Manner
☐ Possessives and Possessive Pronouns

Writing

☐ Describe a room in your home.
☐ Describe how an animal moves.
☐ Describe something you own.
☐ Writing Workshop: Write a Description

Listening and Speaking

☐ Speech

Name ______________________ Date __________

Vocabulary

A. Write the word that completes each sentence.

Sight Words

around
world
warm

Story Words

vegetables
cabbage
tofu

1. I like ______________ weather.
2. My mother makes ______________ soup.
3. Let's take a walk ______________ the pond.
4. There are many different cultures in the ______________ .

B. Circle words from the boxes.

5. All kinds of vegetables grow around the world.
6. We ate warm tofu and vegetables for lunch.

Phonics

A. Write *ir, ur,* or *er* to complete each word.

1. b ____ d
2. n ____ se
3. summ ____
4. g ____ l
5. sh ____ t

B. Circle the word that has the same *-r* sound as in *girl*.

6.	date	dirt	11.	birth	bark
7.	purr	play	12.	first	fire
8.	nerve	nest	13.	her	here
9.	fur	far	14.	bride	firm
10.	burn	born	15.	stir	stick

Name ______________________ Date __________

Think It Over

Reread to tell about the story.

My name is Bayo. My home is in Nigeria. It is hot and dry there.

I like to eat warm bread with meat and rice. Yams, soups, and stews are things I eat, too.

I like to play tag with my friends. I chase them, and I run as fast as I can.

A. Answer the questions.

1. Where does Bayo come from?

2. What does she like to eat?

3. What kind of a girl do you think she is?

B. Write a sentence to answer each question about Tori.

Pen Pals
Who is Tori writing to?
What does her name mean?
Where does Tori live?
When does she fly her kite?
Why does she want you to send a note?

Name ______________________ Date __________

Grammar: Capitalization

Use **capital letters** for proper nouns.

Use capital letters for days of the week, months, and holidays.

Underline the proper nouns in each sentence. Make a list of the words.

Example: The plane flew to Mexico.

1. Mr. Hart gave us a book.
2. Kevin likes music.
3. Memorial Day is in May.
4. We'll visit Canada this summer.

Proper Nouns

Mexico

1. ______________
2. ______________
3. ______________ ______________
4. ______________

Writing

Read the paragraph. It is missing five periods. Add the periods.

I would like to visit California. California is a very big state I would hike in the mountains I could also swim in the Pacific Ocean California has big cities and small towns There are all kinds of things to do

Name ______________________ Date __________

Vocabulary

A. Circle five vocabulary words in the Word Search.

S	W	E	D	R	B
W	O	R	L	D	E
O	O	H	W	H	T
U	N	D	E	R	T
L	L	S	H	U	E
D	Y	A	V	L	R

Sight Words

would

better

only

under

Story Words

continent

students

B. Write the word that completes each sentence.

1. I like milk ______________ than orange juice.
2. There are eighteen ______________ in my class.
3. Asia is a big ______________ .
4. Look ______________ the chair for the cat.

Phonics

A. Write the word that names the picture.

1.  ____________

2.  ____________

3.  ____________

4.  ____________

B. Write the letter or letters to complete each word.

5.  ____ m

6.  ____ ark

7.  ____ arden

8.  ____ ard

Name ______________________ Date __________

Think It Over

Reread to tell about the story.

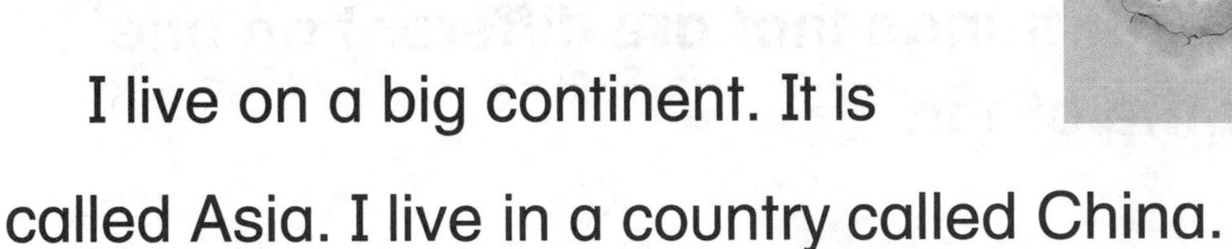

I live on a big continent. It is called Asia. I live in a country called China.

My flag has only two colors. It is red with yellow stars. One star is big. The other stars are not big.

A. Answer the questions.

1. Where does this boy live?

   a. Europe **c.** Africa

   b. Asia **d.** Australia.

2. What colors are on the flag of China?

   ____

3. Look at the map on this page. Is Hong Kong north or south of Shanghai? ______________

B. Think of the place where you live. Think of another place like the ones you read about in the story. Put things that are alike in the middle. Put things that are different on one side or the other.

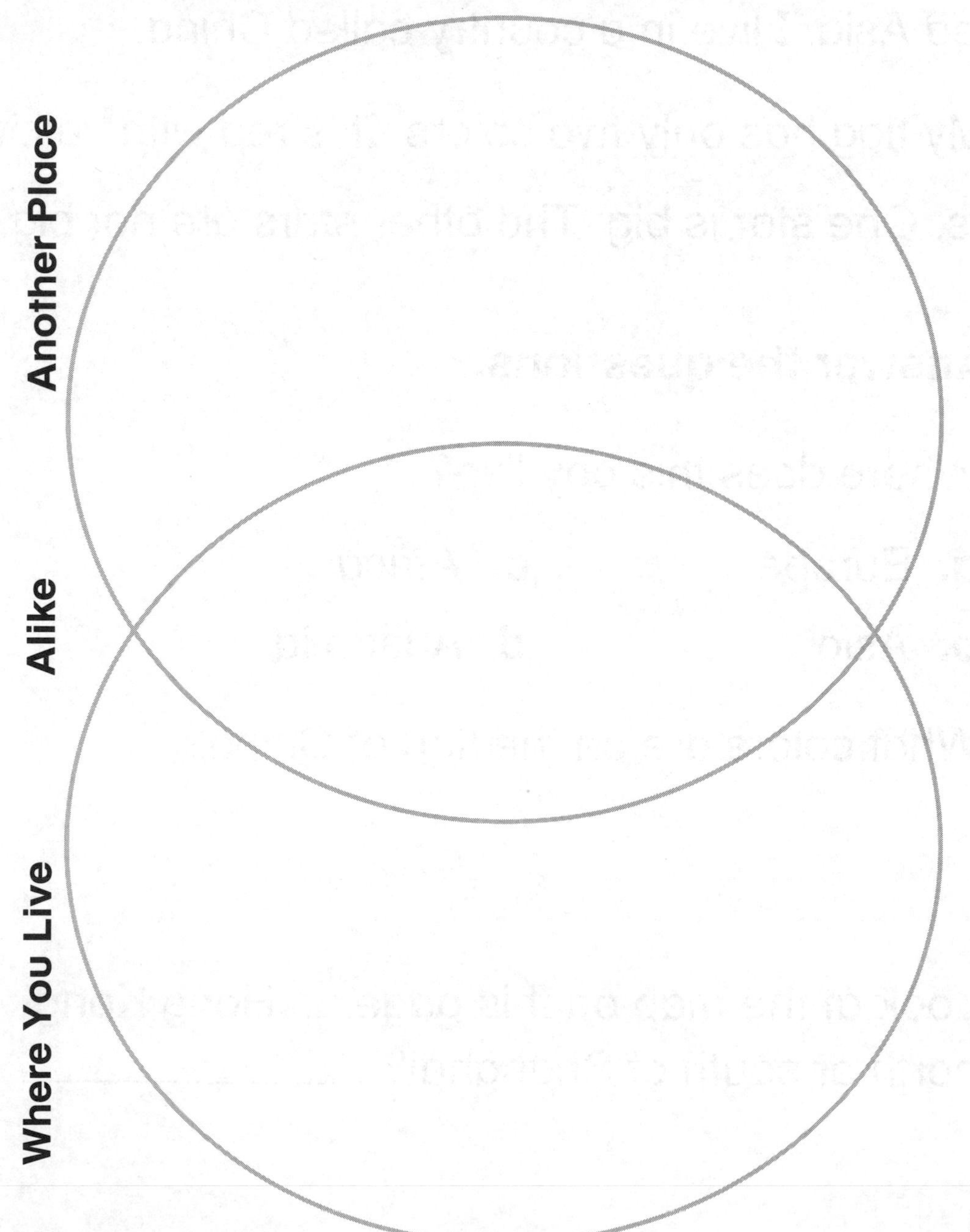

Name ______________________ Date __________

Grammar: Infinitive

Use the **infinitive** to talk about a verb without time. Use *to* + the main verb.

Write a sentence to answer the question. Use the infinitive.

Example: What do you like to eat?
I like to eat pizza.

1. What do you like to do?

____

2. What do you want to learn?

____

3. Where would you like to go?

____

4. What would you like to hear?

____

Writing

Read the paragraph. Circle each proper noun that needs a capital letter. Write the words in the list.

joe went to visit uncle max. Uncle Max is a cook. Joe would like to be a cook, too. They went to the parkside restaurant on sunday. Aunt helen met them there. They had a wonderful dinner!

Proper Nouns

Joe

1. ____________

2. ____________

3. ____________

4. ____________

Name ______________________ Date __________

Vocabulary

A. Fill in the missing letters to complete each word.

Sight Words

morning
once
work
school

Story Words

moment
different
country

1. morn __________
2. coun __________
3. __________ ce
4. wo__________
5. __________ ment
6. __________ ool
7. differ __________

B. Draw a line to match each word with the *best* clue for it.

8. moment	**a.** the first part of the day
9. different	**b.** a very short time
10. morning	**c.** not alike

Phonics

A. Circle the word that has the same *middle* sound as the picture.

1. farm cork car

2.  corn stone want

3.  stay blond floor

4.  soap score son

B. Draw a line to the word that names the picture.

5. storm

6.  corn

7.  score

8.  floor

Name ______________________ Date __________

Think It Over

Reread to tell about the story.

In the morning, Star reads in her classroom at school. Star likes to share her books with her friends.

Carl likes to each lunch with his friends. Carl has fun throughout the day.

A. Circle the letter of the right answer. Then write the word.

1. In the morning, Star ______________.

   a. writes **c.** reads
   b. plays **d.** cleans up

2. Star likes to share her ______________.

   a. snack **c.** toys
   b. pencils **d.** books

3. Carl likes to eat lunch with his ______________.

   a. friends **c.** family
   b. teachers **d.** teammates

B. Fill in the diagram to compare and contrast your morning with Star's morning. Put things that are the same in the middle. Put things that are different on one side or the other.

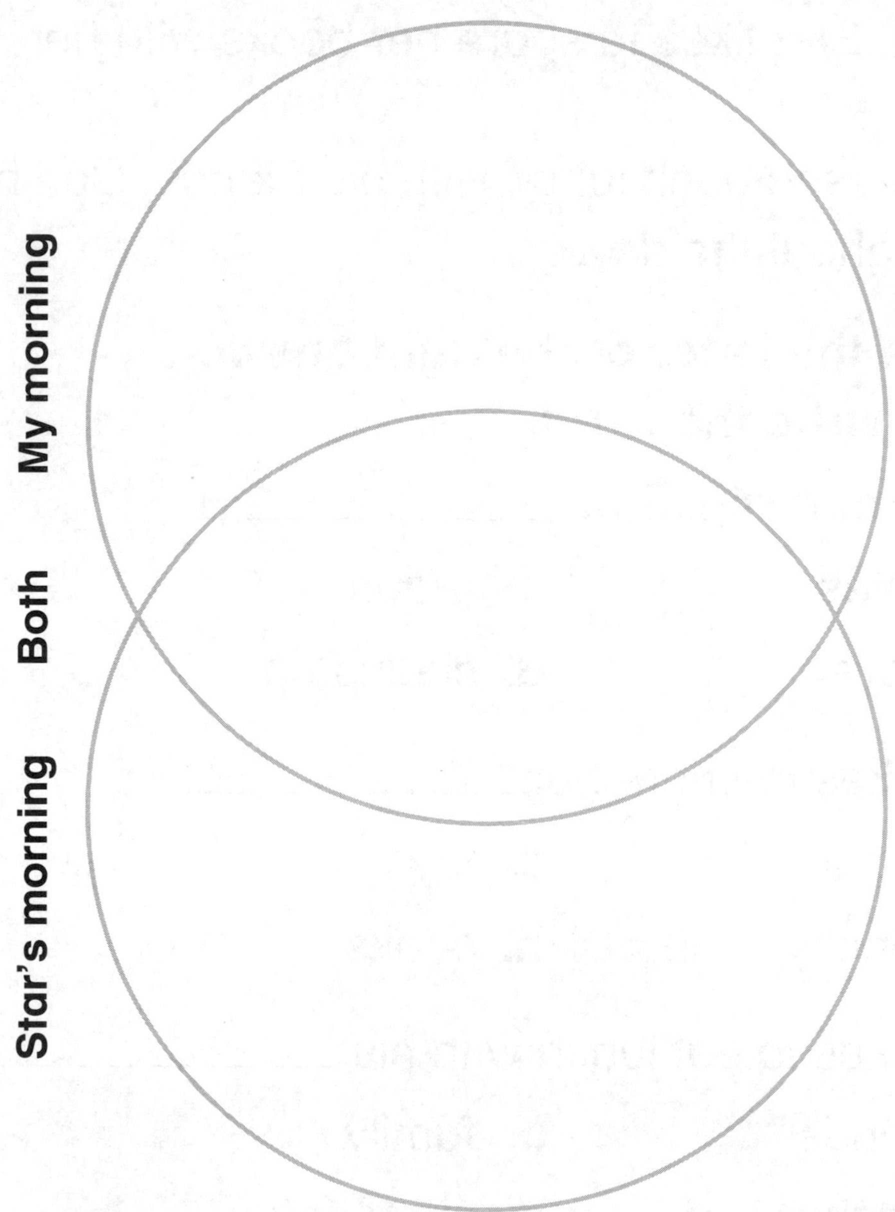

Name ______________________ Date __________

Grammar: Adverbs of Time

Adverbs of time, like *before* and *after*, tell when something happens.

The words *first, then, next,* and *finally* show the order in which things happen.

Choose an adverb from the list. Write the word to complete the sentence.

Example: The show is on Sunday.

first
then
before
after
at
in
on

1. Al makes his lunch ______________ school.
2. We'll go to the bakery ______________ the morning.
3. Let's go to the park ______________ school.
4. ______________, I get out of bed.
5. ______________ I get dressed.
6. The movie begins ______________ 5:00.

Writing

Read the sentences. Circle the error in each one. Write the correct sentences.

School is over on 3:00.

Before I get

home, I walk the dog.

Finally, I have

a snack.

First, I do my homework.

At the

evening, I play a computer game.

Name ____________________ Date __________

Review

Answer the questions after reading Unit 6. You can go back and reread to help find the answers.

1. Circle all the words with the *ir, ur,* and *er* sounds.

My name means bird in Japan.

My dog, Big Skip, and I herd sheep.

2. Who likes to eat warm bread with meat and rice? Circle the letter of the correct answer.

a. Bayo **c.** Tori
b. Lee **d.** Mark

3. In *Schools Around the World,* what can this class do to learn more about students from around the world?

____

4. In *Time at School and at Home,* where does Star live? Circle the letter of the correct answer.

a. Argentina **c.** United States
b. Nairobi **d.** Germany

5. In *Time at School and at Home,* why do you think Dar had a long day?

6. Circle all the words with the *ar* sound.

My name is Mark. This is Star. This is a boy named Carl. Jane and her dad visit a big park.

7. Circle all the words with the *or/ore* sound.

This class would like to learn more about students from around the world.
I work hard for my teacher.

8. What would you like to ask a pen pal? Write three questions.

Name ______________________ Date __________

Writing Workshop: Write a How-To Paragraph

Write a paragraph explaining how to do something. Read Grace's paragraph.

1. **Prewrite** Plan your paragraph. Write the steps in the graphic organizer below. Make sure they are in the correct order.

Step 1
Step 2
Step 3
Step 4
Step 5

2. **Draft** Use your chart to write a first draft.

3. **Revise** Read your draft. Does it explain how to do something? Try to write better sentences.
4. **Edit** Use the Editing Checklist on page 346 of your book to check your paragraph. Correct your writing.
5. **Publish** Make a clean copy of your final draft on a sheet of paper. Share it with the class.

Name ______________________ Date __________

Fluency

A. Read the sentences aloud. Practice saying them as fast as you can with no mistakes.

1. In the snowy winter sun,
   Sally sunburned—not much fun.
2. On the farm or at the park,
   get home safe before it's dark.
3. Thunder, lightning—what a storm!
   Behind our door we're safe and warm.

B. Read each sentence several times. Then cover each one with your hand and try to say it word for word.

1. Peter found a bird's nest in the dirt.
2. Globes and maps show the Arctic circle.
3. At the shore, people swim and play in the sand.

C. Take turns reading the sentences aloud with a partner. Use your finger to follow the words. Read aloud for one minute. Count your words.

Schools around the World tells what it is like for 10
students in their schools and homes. Chun 17
is from China. He works hard in school and 26
helps his mom and dad at home. Ande is from 36
Kenya, and he likes school work better than 44
his chores. Marco is from Brazil. The hot sun 53
shines, the palm trees grow, and Marco plays 61
on the shore. The students learn about each 69
other. 70

D. Read to your teacher, friends, or family.

Name ______________________ Date __________

Learning Checklist

Word Study and Phonics

- ☐ Suffixes
- ☐ R Controlled Vowels: *ir, er, ur*
- ☐ R Controlled Vowel: *ar*
- ☐ R Controlled Vowels: *or, ore*

Reading Strategies

- ☐ Use Visuals
- ☐ Find Main Idea and Details
- ☐ Make Connections

Grammar

- ☐ Capitalization
- ☐ Infinitive
- ☐ Adverbs of Time

Writing

- ☐ Write about a country.
- ☐ Write about what you would like to do when you grow up.
- ☐ Write about what happens on a typical school day.
- ☐ Writing Workshop: Write a How-To Paragraph

Listening and Speaking

- ☐ Demonstration